Apocalypse on the Linoleum

Josette Akresh-Gonzales

LILY POETRY REVIEW BOOKS

"It's all right to talk about the new Jerusalem, but one day, God's preacher must talk about the new New York, the new Atlanta, the new Philadelphia, the new Los Angeles, the new Memphis, Tennessee. This is what we have to do."
— Dr. Martin Luther King, Jr., *I've Been to the Mountaintop*

"What if, instead of arguing about whether or not God exists, we take a look at *us?*"
— Rabbi Toba Spitzer, *God Is Here*

TABLE OF CONTENTS

MOTHERHOOD IN THE ANTHROPOCENE

Whales Keep Carbon Out of the Atmosphere

her body becomes a parachute under water / fond and dark
like solace / I am convinced my sons will find some living
amid the mild currents / humid air

some scientists radioed a vessel / turned out to be a research ship
dragging an array of underwater air guns
and the whales / sent into suicidal dashes / beachward

humpbacks / especially when diving / push oxygen
to the surface / blue their flippers / disappear and sound
and we wonder / how we'll come up for gulps of air

I Remember Wells of Nausea Worse Than Pain

Trying to decide if we should get our son a phone —
my belly button still popped out forever because of him —

seems like all sixth graders get one by Christmas,
but we were going to hold out until seventh at least,

maybe when his voice begins to crack
open his childhood like split wood, grinning.

His dad says, *Why buy him a ticket to misery?*
Everyone we know wants to shoot themselves —

I remember the cool flavor and smell of the ceramic
sink as I pressed my palms on it during a contraction.

Always on, selfies, the endless texting and commenting
and liking and congratulating. The porn

and the paroxetine. How young should he start shutting down
his ability to speak to another person?

I remember when I got my own phone, in seventh,
talked every afternoon to Sara and Jane and Michael,

an imprint of buttons on my cheek, twirling the cord
around my fingers, all the way down the hall.

The Dolls' House at Windsor Castle

pretend Facebook doesn't exist
      even though its little   red dots

punctuate your brain in   exquisite   exclamation-
      point fantasies.   in context   Google ways to listen

to a son   whose small sad face is
      a tinfoil reflection   of your own.

the last white rhino   has died.
      search the front page of the internet

for signs of us.   crunchy brown weeds underfoot
      in the backyard.   the BBC documentary

broadcasts a lithe posh woman in a red knit dress
      caressing   a miniature wooden chest

made for the baby queen.   in your living room   Jupiter's
      spot vanishes   snow drifts against the window pane

shotty memories of a day in June when   at the top
      of a mountain in Vermont   you took a huge bite

of a salami sandwich   and rested your back on a flat rock
      while your son   whose melancholy is

your own   played Minecraft at his grandma's desktop.   so
      translate this: the colors of the hideaway garden

are even better than
                the real thing.

What I Meant

I was looking through old photo albums
with my five-year-old son, and he pointed to one
and said, *I've never seen you look that way.*

What way, I said. Young?

*So happy — that look — you never look the way
you're looking in that picture.*

Sure, I said, you've seen me smiling
like that. I smile with you all the time.

No, he said, *that's a different sort of look.*

OK, I said, wow. You know, that
picture was taken before I had you,
before I became a mom.

I made you unhappy, he said.

No, no, I said.
That's not what I meant.

The Earth

why I brought life into the world / the cruel world
the Anthropocene / I do not regret // the uterine language

a mother tongue / that urges us / to procreate // mass extinctions
the result of asteroids / but greenhouse gasses caused all but

the one that killed the dinosaurs / 252 million years ago
97% of all life on Earth died // I do not regret // right now

we exhaust carbon with power lines / beef cattle / cut rainforest
the rate accelerating / a slate-wiping is due // I do not regret

irrational panic mobs / sober-minded scientists / credentialed
and tenured / few of them inclined to alarmism / quietly apocalyptic

because mother tongue / I do not regret // what right do I have
the seething shores at Bangladesh / the burning forests of California

Mad Mad Mad Mad

Oh, my god we *did*
fly to Tuscany
and escape the world,
with its tortured whistleblowers
in solitary
and its fucking nutty wars
that go on and on
because we can't
name them right —
and we held the tips of our fingers
on our nipples and hummed
LA LA LA
to its twisted confessions,
confiscated phones and computers
of marathon bombers
who went to the same gym as
fellow Chechens —
and we threw a middle finger up
at the world to come,
its degrading prescriptions
between the lips of doctors
on slips of Rx letterhead
placebos more often than not
with our bacteria mutating
to keep up with
new drugs —
we forgot all that
and blinked in awe at
the cliffs of grapevines
bodies in the mirror still wet from the sea,
knocked the rocks glasses over
on the bedside tables
just like Don Draper
and his marionette of the month.

I Said Screen Time Is Over in One More Minute

add it to my list of things I lose every year / should buy stock in
gloves cards keys phones chargers socks

that day I skated backwards and my son forwards
on the ice / knees and snow we / slick fall

we could not gather the effort
to go back / fetch the mittens

my son / now a dozen years into life / confides
soft-voiced / his hands crossed on his shoulders / eyes watering

looks sideways at me as I lie down next to him
says crossly the unthinkable / *I shouldn't be alive*

maybe next year / in the future / six minutes from now
socks will regenerate from sockets in drywall

Shrouds Are Made Without Pockets

Needle and thread, scissors and other notions —
do you know anyone who still mends their clothes
or polishes their shoes anymore? I'm not exempt —
my children's sneakers, every six months, trash.

Yet I bought this shoe-shining kit — two stiff brushes,
felt cloth, carbon black polish of wax and lanolin,
volatile spirits — a single can lasts several months
or years even.

          And this morning I unearthed my sewing kit
that had lost its needle-threader and squinted, licked
the end of the blackest thread and stuck it through the eye
of the needle — one millimeter away from nothing.

My children ask, *Why did you have us if the world is ending?*
I answer — because the world *isn't* ending — because *all our stuff,*
even these threadbare yoga pants and scuffed penny loafers, will last,
darned and shined — until graffitied walls

                          crawl with vines
                          in the ruins
                          of hurricane bloom.

We Look Up "The Reckless Decade"

My son distrusts people who are happy   all the time
members and children smug   at the synagogue event

paper plates   disposable cutlery. Historians will find
our Laminate era   forming a plastic   merry layer.

What did people do before sponges?   my son asks
Were their dishes even clean? Reddit says: rags

empty flour sacks stiff horsehair brushes even sand.
A tub for scrubbing. A bowl for rinsing.   I read this

to my son who has a general distrust of mirth!   who
avoids   circles   service   penance   and   song.

I say   another word for   God can be my stubborn
optimistic method of blowing my nose   into a plain

white hanky   I throw in the wash   over and over.

Earthquake Sensors Record Unprecedented Drop in Human Activity Due to Pandemic

I lifted up my pregnant belly
with my hands
and placed it
on the body pillow
and wrapped my legs around it
and grabbed my man's
two fists
and told him
to push them into my back
just above my ass
told him take this pressure off
but he rolled
the other way
and Americans said
if fracking
causes birth defects
and cancer it's OK
because
we love cheap gas
and I couldn't fall asleep
for *hours* thinking about how
the biggest fracking earthquake
was a mag 4 in Texas
and the weight of my abdomen
rolled heavy with cargo
an elbow in New York
a heel in California
a back in the Dakotas
for hours a finger poking
under the Florida Keys
and energy released in waves
causes the ground to shake
and my palms pick up
the signal

Placenta

I lie on my back on my sheets on my bed —
the baby a regret, the pains a regret.
What was full inside is now outside, on my breast.
The baby slick with blood, the blood like a river,
the fluid that circulates, carrying food and water and breath
and bringing away waste from all parts.

Tributaries, thick with brick-red
sediment, clay figurines,
mud that sifts down with the gravity that is my birthright.
The baby's hair sticks to his head.
His minute-old eyes come up, dark gray,
to look at me for the first time.

And he suckles then, almost without my knowing.
My nipples the size of his mouth.
Forming an O, his lips open to swallow,
and he brings on the third stage of labor,
the womb caving in to deliver my placenta.

And the ache of the tightening uterus,
the organ that had held and nourished him,
draws together and breaks its betrothal to me,
pulls its stitches out, unknitting itself.
One midwife cleans the baby's head with warm cloth,
the other squats between my legs.

The afterbirth comes, flat and heavy, slugging down
between my thighs into an aluminum mixing bowl.
There are veins and membranes and farmers,
dark grass, brown bulls, cords of wood, storms and rain.

The pain of the birth canal ripping — as his elbow caught —
had been astounding.
I'm suddenly awake to it, sharp —
needle pierces the lips like memory. Only not as clear as it had been.

Baby sleeping and clean,
a midwife threads my perineum shut,
the puckered tissue between anus and birth canal,
a border mended between warring tribes.

The midwife turns the placenta over
in her hands — red and silent.
Her eyes remain low, concentrating.
She is searching for flaws.
I may not be ready. It is perfect.

I Hope Your Birthday Is So Beautiful, It Hurts to Look at It

In the late afternoon at the foot of the Green Mountains,
Rachel, in the shade of her porch, picks a handful of beans
the length of her palm — religion of summit and breath,

barbeque and a good dog and beer and acres of thigh-high grass
touched by the first draft of evening. A sunlit breeze lunges
across the hay field. We stand around, breathing.

My mother's obsessed with this story — a woman
who was beat up in her nursing home by an aide,
frustrated by the shower, several red knots on her forehead.

I picture a nurse sleeping in the room my parents fill with the *Times*,
her coral uniform behind the door. Rachel comes back and says,
"I grew these beans from seed," and I picture my dad, my earliest

memory of him in a wheelchair — he knows what it's like
to have a small woman lift him up by the armpits.
I blurt out that we could say the *Shehecheyanu*. Why I felt

like praying I don't know — the warm, soft shine on the field, the big sky,
the wet crunch of the green beans — but that's something my mom
would insist: "Let's say the *Shehecheyanu*." Her *Chabadnik* traditions,

her city, her Israel, her kashrut. No, I'm thinking of the last seeds
buried safe inside the Arctic Circle, our flooded future, this heat,
and under my breath, my parents, this sustained note on my tongue —

shehecheyanu v'ke'yi'mah'nu v'hee'gee'ah'nu la'zman ha'zeh.

"Pain Scares Me Stupid," She Said

A tumor the size of a football.
The fluid starts to build up in her belly
and she has to lie down on the crackling paper
to watch it pump out into dozens of glass bottles,
but at the end she is weightless, shaking out her wet wings.
Her daughter is there to hold her elbow,
and together they pick up the prescription at CVS,
place it in a nightstand drawer for now.
When it's time, she swills down the self-killing fluid
and thinks aloud, "The room is swirling. This is so easy.
This should be so easy for everyone.........Mama..."
Then the camera turns to the shadows
on the curtains and we understand that she is silent
because she is dead.

After watching this documentary,
you are not only convinced, you are a convert:
you seek out stories on NPR about palliative care,
find one about how, in Uganda, women with breast cancer
scream in their huts, alone, not knowing about morphine
unless they live in the city or near a clinic
and another one about training American doctors
to be more compassionate.
What are they so scared about?
Addiction and abuse, they say.
You see yourself
with a crate of signatures,
your hands bloody with paper cuts.
You see your sister and mother (two doctors)
fighting over Right to Die until
you can't speak anymore.

In the car on the way home from work
you daydream about a bad diagnosis,
decide to move to Oregon
now, before it's too late, or
if that's impossible, how you'd locate
some punk teenager to sell you heroin,
just in case.

Long Suffering

Today a paramedic asks himself if he has PTSD, or if he's just down.
Held a boy, lost his leg, bled buckets, but yes,
he's, weeks later, getting by,
every day a little easier.
What do we expect of him?
To pop out of the ground and turn green?
To, a second later in time-lapse,
tendril over to the nearest root and climb?
And my mother-in-law, who lost her father not too long ago,
who nurses her mother now after heart surgery almost took her too,
is supposed to "stay positive"
and stake her phototropic efforts, even at night
when her eyelids fold under like bloodroot blooms
and turn inward
to grieve, the dew drops on her cheeks betray her.
In the end I want them all to be sad,
actually in the "pathetic" sense and in the "end of the road,"
heads-not-resting-on-their-pillows sense, but pound and suffer.
I want my husband's mother to say how hard it is,
to say *It's been three years since my father passed,*
and it hasn't gotten any easier.
I want to hear the medic's voice break,
weeping at his wheel at first light,
when he in turn listens to an interview with the boy's mother
on the radio, the boy who will never walk again.
The radio host's voice crisp
as the paramedic catches his Adam's apple in his throat.
His tense shoulders square off as he steps out of the truck,
his work boots thud on the pavement,
the rubber of his heels a cool shock to stop the shudder of his grief.
He has a job to do, a life to go back to living.
You'll never hear the host say *Give it a year,* or even
That's as it should be.

JERUSALEM

I Buried the Workweek

Sometimes I feel like I'm at the funeral of our way of life: I've buried the workweek and that buoyant uplift on Friday afternoon, but also weekends, podcasts, the dollar, water-bottle islands floating in acid ocean currents, Hondas and Toyotas and Fords, hurricane-surge in subway tunnels, white-sand beaches and diamond rings, the Patriots, tomato pickers tied to trucks, Netflix streaming, session beer in cans. Retirement.

I have not showered; I have covered all the mirrors; I have left the front door open for the ten people who will say the kaddish with me. They don't have to knock. We all remember Marvel comics fondly, and when we hug tears well up over the end of Google and Disney. I'm sitting on a low stool and someone is bringing me hard-boiled eggs and lentils. People kiss my cheek and tell me they are so sorry. *Baruch dayan emet,* they say, a ritual blessing, incomprehensible in its literal translation *blessed is the judge of truth* or maybe it's actually *blessed is the true judge.*

It's like our way of life is still here, somehow, I say. They see I'm kneading brown bread dough on the kitchen table and remind me not to cook or dance or laugh. I can feel the grain of the wood in the table and say, *I might need to take a nap.*

On the seventh day, I'm sitting on my stool and someone says, *Get up,* and that is the sign to me that the shivah is done.

There Was a Man Named Job

Every time I go to an American funeral,
I think, WOW,
the Jews really get death.
I came naked from my mother's womb,
and I will be naked when I leave.
This is from *The Book of Job,* which traditional Jews read
to the body as it fumes unembalmed
in the cool night air.
Maybe we've always read this, a scroll
some claim is the oldest book in the world —
older than *Genesis!*
These Americans trying to come up with something new,
going beyond wakes and makeup and flowers
to arranging the dead in scenes that resemble life —
say, Uncle Rich sitting in the kitchen
on a chair at the table
drinking a pint glass of Busch.
When three of Job's friends heard of the tragedy he had suffered,
they got together and traveled from their homes to comfort and console him.
There's not many embalmers who could do that — it's quite technical.
And some asking for "green" burials.
Let the day of my birth be erased,
and the night I was conceived.
Just listen to that.
We Jews don't fuck around with death.
If you're a Jew and you die, three people sit and watch you
Curse that day for failing to shut my mother's womb,
for letting me be born to see all this trouble
and your limbs shrouded in linen, boxed in pine —
you're already decomposing in the heat.
If only God would speak;
if only he would tell you what he thinks!
That first night, the three that watch
are called *shomer* (guard or watchman, but really it's about honor) for

The poor must go about naked, without any clothing.
They harvest food for others while they themselves are starving.
They press out olive oil without being allowed to taste it,
and they tread in the winepress as they suffer from thirst.
So in the morning when you tilt topsoil on the box in the ground,
it's not too far from tilling or harvesting,
and the scientific fact is right there in front of you,
holy in its brown wormy shovelful,
holy in knowing that's where you'll go, too —
that's where it helps to remember the words of Job
as he cursed יהוה   THE UNIVERSE
and יהוה   THE ETERNAL CHAOS ALL AROUND US
responded:
Have you comprehended the expanse of the earth?
Is it by your wisdom that the hawk soars
and spreads her wings toward the south?

Meleke, The Royal Stone, a White
Coarse Crystalline Limestone

a teenager at the Wailing Wall　　　I pushed a pinched scrap into a crack

the width of God　　a millimeter thick

handwritten　　　a note that asked God/wall

to quarry back from stone　　　my father's legs

I bent my forehead to the sandstone cool　　　and wept　　God/self

a cistern in the quarry　　in the evening my friends and I　　　swayed

singing　　*let brothers sit togethe*r　　　the desert breeze　dry as dust

the Jerusalem air　　crown-daisy cupped faces　　the way it sifts around our skin

looking back I know　　　childish melodies　*the whole world*

a very narrow bridge　our foolish glow　　our cheeks like domes　shining

shevet achim　　*and the main thing*　　*is to have no fear at all*

but the cobbled　　　　streets/God　and crowds　*gam yachad*　and reflections

in gold　　inhaled　　exhaled prayer

Mandatory Palestine

It is 1920 at San Remo and the boundaries of the mandated territories
    are not precisely defined

It is 2018 and I am streaming videos of the border and the tear gas
    and the tears and the blood

It is 1996 and I am holding hands with a boy in the golden sunset the
    desert air blooming

It is 1986 and my class and I are wearing blue and white in Manhattan
    at the Israeli Day Parade

It is 1976 and my parents are strolling in the West Bank and an Arab
    boy is throwing rocks

It is 1948 and four hundred Arab villages are under attack and are
    forced to evacuate, never to return to their green olive groves

It is 1917 in the Ottoman Empire and the Turks are about to lose
    Palestine to the British Mandate

It is 2018 and a string of Palestinian protesters, hands held tight,
    shout and push at the gate

It is 1996 and we are outside the hostel in Jerusalem because a boy left
    his backpack in a bathroom stall

It is 1991 and Saddam launches scud missiles into Tel Aviv where my
    cousins pull on gas masks

It is 1976 and my parents could walk the mosaic tiles of the mosque at
    the hilltop holding hands

It is 1947, on the world map within the tiny arrow of Palestine a speck
of white where the UN proposes to hold Jerusalem as trustee

It is 1920 and a small boy and his sister have left the orphanage in
Jerusalem in a ship bound for New York

It is 2018 and I watch the live feed of a Palestinian baby bleeding in
her father's lap

It is 1996 and we gather at Rabin's stone, heads down, placing pebbles
on his grave, crying *who would shoot him*

It is 1973 and the Yom Kippur War closed round like a noose,
Egyptians crossing the Suez Canal, Syrians rushing down from the
top of the Golan Heights

It is 1948 and my grandmother is pregnant with her third baby boy,
another New York Jew, her Moisheleh, my dad

It is 1918 and only a fraction of the orphans in Jerusalem find shelter,
my grandpa Sam among them

It is 2018 and at least sixty people are dead at the border, hundreds
more fist-sized holes at the exit

It is 1996 and

It is 1973 and

It is 1948 and

It is 1922 and

It is 2018

The Seven O'clock News

Gaza is a human rubbish heap that everyone would
rather ignore. Sometimes the poison gets out.
—The Economist, *May 19, 2018*

We sang a song about Jerusalem in chorus in 5th grade,
        a folk song

"Yerushalayim Shel Zahav" — it's running through my head now,
        an earworm on top of the news of the simple
        announcement to move the U.S. embassy to Jerusalem

A promise, to red-state evangelicals, a bonfire
        redemption, the second coming

Jesus Christ

I heard "Yerushalayim Shel Zahav" on a scratched record
        my parents received on their El-Al flight to Israel in 1976

A candle on the cover, orange and gold, rotated
        with Simon and Garfunkel's rendition of "Silent Night"
        layered atop the Vietnam War news
        chilling even then, when

I had no idea

In the Kingdom of God There Are No Accidents

a found poem from "Israel Captures the Heart of Texas,"
The Torch, *Christians United for Israel, Winter 2017*

On the plane home, Diana listened to the stories of more IDF soldiers. One young man described how he asked his commanding officer to paint his face for war and make sure he came home, even if he died in battle.

Diana wept. She realized that she'd allowed fear to keep her from doing some of the things God had told her to do for Israel, and suddenly she felt in her spirit a simple but compelling message: Even though you fear, put the blood of Jesus on you.

Salaam

My friends, I have placed my forehead
        on the woven prayer mat in a mosque

And I have drunk tea in tiny, heavy glasses
        cross-legged on a Persian rug in a living room

At the mosque I pulled on a long cotton skirt
        from a bin at the door

And at the break of the Ramadan fast I said
        salaam to my neighbor's (my best friend's)
        mother's friends and sisters and air-kissed
        cheeks like French sophisticates

In America my father and her father could play
        backgammon with no hard feelings they said
        welcome come in sit down have some tea

In the entrance to the mosque in a dusty town
        north of Jerusalem I heard the tongues
        of my father's father's father and lowered my knees

Next to the hot strong tea always honey sweet saffron
        and rose pastries on a delicate white plate

In Europe, Mothers Enjoy
Two Years of Maternity Leave

Gun deaths are rare and infant mortality is lower than here,
and when the high-speed rail workers strike
the whole city shuts down.

I could move there with my family and learn the language —
in the middle of the night, that thought —
I don't really have a home town.

The closest thing I have is Brooklyn.
The boardwalk, and the pop–smack of men playing handball
under the boardwalk, their backs sweaty and all shades of brown,

Grandma changing out of her flowered bathing suit
right on the beach, seagulls and AM radio,
guys pushing carts chanting over the ocean and the people

Get yer fudgie wudgies here!
Get yer cold beer here!
Ice cold soda here!

But there's still Yiddish in Williamsburg,
in the southern corner of the neighborhood
a few streets sounding like the Lower East Side

in the early 1900s, when my grandma was born in a toilet
and learned what a carrot tasted like
at public school while her brothers manned the paper stand.

She told me the only carrots she knew were "soup carrots,"
and after she died, I closed the door on Brooklyn —
maybe I wasn't a New Yorker anymore.

New York Jew

There are kosher chickens in the
   supermarket freezer section

so we plant trees in the Negev

There are weddings officiated
   by a priest and a rabbi

so we send clothes for the poor
     Soviet refugees

Our taxes are low

so we import prayer books from Israel

Public schools are closed on
   Yom Kippur

so we are allowed to complain about the
   heat on the tarmac at Ben Gurion

Country clubs' swimming pools
   don't forbid us

so we import etrogim from Eretz
   Yisrael — you can't grow them here

Our temple pews are mostly empty

so we write checks to AIPAC
   and pro-Israel politicians

We have a first-rate Holocaust
   museum in DC

so we buy Teva sandals and
   SodaStream seltzer

Whenever neo-Nazis knock over some
   gravestones in New Jersey the news
   covers it

so we buy Dead Sea mud online

The Cleanup Crew at the Western Wall

Twice a year, the custodians of the Western Wall brush the thousands of papers crushed into cracks between stones and sweep up the plaza. I don't think anyone believes that the prayers are somehow defunct once the paper is discarded. Whether or not there is a God to receive them is up to each person, don't you think? A story that before the ark, the temple, God was lonely, and once the people built a place for God, God dwelt there. Once a person's prayers are spoken/written and said/placed, I would guess the person praying feels that their urgent message is sent. In the story, when God was alone, God spoke...and God listened. I remember the times I scribbled a note and stuck it in the Western Wall, and I wondered how a fresh crowd of people each day could find space to squish their crumpled gratitude and self-pity into the wall. From the Middle Ages until the British Mandate forbade it, pilgrims drove nails into the wall and marked the wall with painted palm prints. In the story, if you are in the right place at the right time, you may be lucky enough to overhear God speaking to God's self...Creation echoing in Creation like your child's voice calling in a canyon. It also occurred to me at the time when I prayed at the wall that if there was a God, the mind of God would have to be able to easily expand to hold all the words in the universe, much less the spoken ones, much less the written ones, much less the high-priority ones scribbled on tiny scraps of paper and stuffed into both wide and thin spaces between the hewn stones of the Western Wall. I think about how, all over the planet, we face Jerusalem, because our people built this place for God, and God must see that we are facing God's face when we pray. And in the story, the canyon echoes/God and the voice/God and the ears/God and time/God and we/God enter and clean up and enter and clean up and enter the place in the story where God is.

Inquisition

In 1492, my ancestor Rabbi Isaac ben Abraham Akrish
left Spain with all his books and ended up in the Ottoman
Empire — he was known in his time as "Pathetic Akrish"

after a horrible accident left him a cripple in both legs —
a strange echo of what happened to my dad, who has walked
with crutches since he came down with Guillain-Barré syndrome.

Rabbi Akrish was a writer and editor, and
he left Spain with all his books, spent some years tutoring
a rich man's son in Cairo and settled in Constantinople.

Somehow his descendants made their way to Hebron and
then my grandpa Sam (when I knew him) had tan skin,
a cigarette in his mouth, and a fishing pole in his hand.

The Front Gates of the Jewish Graveyard in Cairo

The gates of Bassatine were locked
with a heavy chain and the graveyard
was surrounded by a wall.

It was too high to climb,
but along the far side
I spotted a makeshift earthen ramp.

I was halfway up the ramp when
someone started shouting at me
from inside the graveyard.

It's closed, he said, *the cemetery is closed.*

I'm Jewish, I shouted down.

Although his face softened somewhat,
he still wouldn't let me in.

Talk to the rabbi, he said, *you need an appointment.*

City of Gold

when "Yerushalayim Shel Zahav" came out in 1967

borne on the evening wind with the sound of bells

guitar and soprano   clear   bright   I didn't know

at that time   the Hashemite Kingdom of Jordan   owned the Old City

banned Jews from the Old City and the rest of Jerusalem east of it

Jerusalem of gold, of bronze and light   even the cisterns under the bus stop holy

Jews lost their homes   and possessions   and became refugees

all Jews   barred from returning

holy sites   the wall?   damaged stone of kings with stones

how have the cisterns dried out?

only three weeks after Shemer released the song

the Six-Day War broke out   they dropped leaflets from jets

in the slumber of trees and stone   imprisoned in her dream

morale-boosting battle cry of the IDF   Palestinian families homeless

the market square is empty   let me not forget you, Jerusalem

Shemer herself sang it for the troops   making them among the first

in the world to hear it   and she added a verse   for victory

we have returned   the shofar calls on the Mount

The Orphans in Jerusalem

My grandfather Shmuel knew only that he was born
in Hebron between the day of atonement and the season of our joy
and that he and his sister Sarah had some uncles in New York.

Their parents — Mazel had died of cholera and Abraham had died
a soldier for the Turks — and so the children spoke Ladino
and Hebrew and maybe Arabic at the orphanage in Jerusalem.

In Jerusalem the homeless children the motherless the fatherless
the children of the Great War the cholera the genocide the famine
a hundred thousand or a hundred and fifty thousand children.

What is an orphanage? What did they wear? What did they eat?
Who paid for their schooling? Were they beaten? Did the streets'
golden stone clack under shoes or smack with bare feet?

Unreal

C, now leading my local liberal activist group, posted a meme from *8 Bit Communism: What's your favorite place that isn't real?* Fantasy land and sea map of Hyrule. Mushroom Kingdom of Mario Brothers. Vice City in neon pink letters. And Israel. You work to breathe. You feel the hearts stop of the millions of people. Your cousins and their cousins. All those U.S. tax dollars, going…where, exactly? M, the mother of a friend of my son's, asks me while we kill time walking around the soccer field, *So, what is going on in Gaza? I don't understand.* The deep breath, the telling about the meme and its offense. An hour of summarizing the last century as I clip-hop next to her long legs which are speedwalking us out of range of hearing of the kids then back in their territory. The next day, C shares a story with the world titled, "Make Israel Palestine Again," the little blue privacy icon of our planet next to his post showing only North and South America, and I scroll, keep scrolling and scrolling, beyond the newsfeed, past the suburbs with their black-and-white balls and nets, over the river of small children in their neon shirts, at a distance from the dark-suited U.N. motions, a long way off from the demands of all my breathing and unbreathing kin.

The Trumpet Player

After spending all morning in the children's service,
it turns out to be time for yizkor, but I stay
anyway — this room a home, this hallway a village,
this trash can a landfill, this stage a sanctuary.

No one sat with my mother — God forbid
you should tempt the evil eye —
she had to be there with the old people.
The chanting starts with the voice of the cantor,
whose microphone has a feedback loop,
"May God remember my father, my teacher,"
because my grandpa lanced his mole with a safety pin,
died after the cancer swirled in his blood.
And the pace at which you run
from the squealing loudspeaker
is understandable,
isn't it?

Sound without anyone actually playing,
it reminds me of the people's mic,
how those who can hear, repeat, louder.
In the hall, I tell a friend about Yom Kippur at Occupy, how
I stood up, opened my eyes.
The words I heard in my mouth —
I let them out.
Gone now my honey-sweet wrongs,
whatever I have done —
I cast them into the river.
Mercy for caring deeply about commas
instead of migrant slaves.

This year we decide to break the fast at a bistro table
near the bar at the Lizard Lounge.
I see after ten years

a woman taking off her sweater — a teacher I had —
she used to get all worked up,
arms would go up and over,
a faded sun on her shoulder, really faded —
like any good tattoo that'd earned its place on stage.
She could always tell when I was staring at her.
She taught me how to be in front of a roomful of teenagers
by singing in a punk-rock band
and hosting parties in her yellow house in JP.
She looked back at me from her table and said,
I remember you.
And I said, I have two kids so I've forgotten everything.

Onstage, the trumpet player wets the insides of his cheeks,
takes a deep breath, turns the horn
to his face — his bell a spotlight, his blast an alarm,
his harmony a mitzvah, his flat fifth a broken moan.

The Mechitza

My childhood —
almost impossible to imagine for my husband,
a white guy from Boston.
Wait, he says, *you had to pray behind a partition?*
I say, it's called a mechitza,
and it's about yay high.
Where I went, you daven separately,
boys on one side, girls on the other.
He also can't wrap his head around
those leather boxes on the boys' heads and arms,
black leather straps —
Is that like S&M?
I say, that's tefillin,
the boys learn to wrap it in a particular way,
with a bruchah,
and to kiss the gold lettering on the boxes.
And they wrap it tight, so that when they
bare their arms after davening,
depressions on their skin spiral
up their biceps and along their forehead and temples,
mark them as men.

He and I sit for a moment — him trying to picture this scene
and me, bare-shouldered, trying to remember
the other side.
The mechitza stood there like a rope in a lake
and the teachers were buoys attached to the rope
and we swam around it.
No one said, it will be like this —
you will stay in the back
with your pink and white dresses and your patent leather shoes
and the boys will gather round the Torah
in their black suits, seriously,
and learn to put tefillin.

When the door opened we flocked into
the davening room and found our seats.
In the front of the room, the boys
adjusted their bodies in black pants and collared shirts,
opened their siddurs, embroidered with their names,
volunteered or were called on to lead.

My husband argues, *It must be different now
for girls, even the Orthodox.*
I don't know, I say.

Behind the mechitza, we gossiped,
sometimes followed along —
a naughty girl wore a jean skirt above her knee
and was sent to the office.
Can you even believe that's how it was?
My family practically just got here —
we came smelling of cabbage
and pogroms, lentils and sea salt —
does that make sense?

Skipping Class in the Yeshiva Bathroom

We're just laughing in the girls' bathroom
me and a girl who wanted to practice kissing —
of course we were supposed to be in Rabbi First's class,
of course it was called דינים *(Laws)* —
the bathroom was dingy tile, smelled of pee,
on the wall a laminated poster with
the blessings to say when you've gone to the bathroom:
    בִּרְכַּת אֲשֶׁר יָצַר *(the blessing of fortune)*
and washed your hands:
    עַל נְטִילַת יָדַיִם *(on washing of hands)*

Judy's flat black hair in my palm, our hands between our lips.

She said, "When a man and a woman have sex,
he puts his thing in her thing
and they can get stuck like that forever!"

My laugh has always been a foghorn — I covered it,
my trumpet, and smelled Judy's sweat on my palm,
a minute ago we had been good girls
opening our חומשים *(five books)* to page 54, please read the Rashi
in a loud, clear voice, now we turned to each other
with a stuttering blush and our cheeks pink,
my glasses crashed into her face, the plastic frames bending.

I said: "We should go back we should go back —
we're going to get in trouble,
they're going to call our parents!" —
my giggles rising up in a foam from my stomach,
remembering getting caught kissing a different girl
in my bedroom, my mom's anger poured
over my head ashamed ashamed —

I said: "Rabbi First will send us to the office!"
She said: "OK, OK, lesbo. We'll go back."

Took my hand, pulled open the heavy door, let go —
smell of the school hallway, its waxed floor,
thick-painted concrete walls with taped-up arts & crafts
waving in the breeze we made
running past.

Goy Means Nation

I am sick of reminding the goyim it's Yom Kippur.
What's that one again?
Linen, sneakers, white, the fast with no water —
that's crazy.
Have you ever done that?
I try not to be a stereotype when my sons' soccer games
are scheduled on Yom Kippur — it's so micro I'm not allowed to be lonely
or mad or missing New York
when I have to break the news to him,
after all, what do we expect them — the goyim — to do?
Change the schedule for two out of a hundred?
Only in certain pockets are the schools closed on Yom Kippur
where you can count on maybe a few of the goyim
to know anything about you.
The only things on the top of the hill are the shul and the soccer fields
within earshot of each other,
where by some fluke
the game starts at the same time as services, so
I will follow his inevitable gaze:
just out of reach, the boys
in gray, black, and silver uniforms,
Angel with a kick,
the toe a neon yellow
punts clear
to the sky,
ball and astroturf shine
a lure for a boy to the point of torture.
We will be fasting across from the soccer fields,
singing *Avinu Malkeinu* across from the soccer fields
pleading in the voice of Isaiah: "Behold we fast..." across from the soccer fields —
and my son who loves soccer and does not believe in God?
He will hate my guts.
And I will apologize — but not do t'shuvah —
how can I?

When I am not really sorry, when I know in my gut
that being a Jew is a misery and soccer is
joy
and the sky above
wants to meet him at the goal —
and joy is for the goyim,
otherwise
where will he come from?
On what field will he play
(run and play, go)
but who are his people?
Not the Hasidim who picked joy
but also the ghetto.
He picked defense as his position.
But if he plays soccer on the holiest day of the year
he won't ever know
what defense is.

Letter to My Aunts, Uncles, and Cousins Who Want to Know the Date of My Son's Bar Mitzvah

This weekend I saw two grown men cry:
a man drunk and sick at knowing
his parents had screwed up so badly
they'd fucked up his life
before he was even born
and a man who had lost his old dog —
belly full of cancer
at his kid's third birthday party
while we were opening presents.

My husband helped dig the grave.

Balls hot outside.

The six-year-old girl who loved the dog watched
and asked questions. *Why*
are you digging this hole? Why
are her eyes still open?

Anyway, my father said that you'd been asking if
my son, who's twelve now, was having a bar mitzvah.

No, he's not.

At least not a traditional bar mitzvah —
we will not collect checks in a basket by the door,
the rabbi will not cover the boy's head in her tallis and bless him...

Like a marsh full of birds taking off, feathers splashing,
we too wonder what happened, how a kid
who spoke in full sentences at one and a half
could drop out of Hebrew school at ten, afraid
of the twisted letters and guttural stops.

Prayer felt like a burden or an option to him.

It wasn't something I wanted to force,
muscles flexed and twitching, and of course
we hope you'll come visit sometime —
we sing Shabbos blessings and drink wine
every Friday night — you'd be welcome anytime.

Notes

Earthquake The title is from "Earthquake sensors record unprecedented drop in human activity due to pandemic," *The Washington Post,* July 23, 2020.

I Hope Your Birthday Is So Beautiful, It Hurts to Look at It includes words from the *Shehecheyanu* prayer: …*shehecheyanuv'ke'yi'mah'nu v'hee'gee'ah'nu la'zman ha'zeh,* which are translated "…who has granted us life and sustained us, and allowed/let us [to] arrive at this Time" (Shehecheyanu, Wikipedia, accessed January 29, 2023, at https://en.wikipedia.org/wiki/Shehecheyanu).

There Was a Man Named Job includes the unspeakable name of God, יהוה, or YHVH, and I've offered two possible translations in the margin. One way to read this poem aloud is to say *Yah-weh,* another is to read the English words I've offered, and a third is to say *Adonai,* which means *my Lord* and is what I learned to say in school and synagogue when I encountered this name in prayers or in the Torah.

Meleke The italicized words are from Hebrew songs. The phrase "let brothers sit together" is my English translation of a phrase in Hebrew, *shevet achim gam yachad* from the song "Hiné Ma Tov":
הִנֵּה מַה טּוֹב וּמַה נָּעִים שֶׁבֶת אָחִים גַּם יַחַד.
Its lyrics are the first verse of Psalm 133, which reads, "Behold, how good and how pleasant it is for brethren to dwell together in unity!" (Hine Ma Tov, Wikipedia, accessed January 29, 2023, at https://en.wikipedia.org/wiki/Hine_Ma_Tov).

And "the whole world / a very narrow bridge / and the main thing is to have no fear at all" is my English translation of a phrase in Hebrew,
כָּל הָעוֹלָם כֻּלּוֹ גֶּשֶׁר צַר מְאֹד
וְהָעִיקָר לֹא לְפַחֵד כְּלָל
Kol ha-o-lam ku-lo gesher tzar me'od / V'ha-i-kar lo l'fached klal: "The whole world is a very narrow bridge; / the important thing is not to be afraid." This quote is attributed to Rabbi Nachman of Bratslav (Kol

Ha'Olam Kulo, Zemirot Database, accessed January 29, 2023, at https://www.zemirotdatabase.org/view_song.php?id=220).

City of Gold The italicized words are English translations of lyrics from the Hebrew song "Yerushalayim Shel Zahav," by Naomi Shemer; I've adapted the translation from Shira.net (Yerushalayim Shel Zahav (Jerusalem of Gold), Shira, accessed January 29, 2023, at http://www.shira.net/music/lyrics/yerushalayim-shel-zahav.htm).

The Orphans in Jerusalem Family tree: Mazel and Abraham Akrish are my father's paternal grandparents; Shmuel is my father's father. More information about the orphans of the Ottoman Empire after WWI from "1914-1918-online. International Encyclopedia of the First World War" (Orphans [Ottoman Empire/Middle East], 1914-1918 online. International Encyclopedia of the First World War, last updated April 8, 2015, accessed January 29, 2023, at https://encyclopedia.1914-1918-online.net/article/orphans_ottoman_empiremiddle_east).

Inquisition Family history, including information about Rabbi Akrish, from JewishEncyclopedia.com and other history passed down to me from my father and uncles (AKRISH, ISAAC B. ABRAHAM, JewishEncyclopedia, accessed January 29, 2023, at https://www.jewishencyclopedia.com/articles/1048-akrish-isaac-b-abraham).

The Front Gates of the Jewish Graveyard in Cairo is a found poem from "From Cairo to Kolkata, Traces of a Vibrant Jewish Past," *The New York Times*, June 8, 2018.

In the Kingdom Of God There Are No Accidents is a found poem from "Israel Captures the Heart of Texas," *The Torch,* Christians United for Israel, Winter 2017 (accessed January 29, 2023, at https://www.cufi.org/thetorch/2017-1/).

Acknowledgements

My thanks to the editors of the following publications for their support in publishing my work, sometimes with different titles:

Abstract: "The Seven O'Clock News"
Atticus Review: "Shrouds Were Made Without Pockets"
Bodega Magazine: "Meleke, the Royal Stone, a White Coarse Crystalline Limestone"
Breakwater Review: "The Dolls' House at Windsor Castle"
Clarion: "The Cleanup Crew at the Western Wall" and "The Front Gates of the Jewish Graveyard in Cairo"
Ghost City Review: "Letter to my Aunts, Uncles, and Cousins Who Want to Know the Date of My Son's Bar Mitzvah"
JAMA: "I Remember Wells of Nausea Worse Than Pain"
JuxtaProse: "There Was a Man Named Job"
Lily Poetry Review: "The Earth" and "Goy Means Nation"
Lime Hawk: "Mad Mad Mad Mad"
Literary Orphans: "'Pain Scares Me Stupid,' She Said"
Love's Executive Order: "Mandatory Palestine"
Many Loops: "Salaam," "New York Jew," and a republication of "The Cleanup Crew at the Western Wall"
MAYDAY: "I Hope Your Birthday Is So Beautiful, It Hurts to Look at It"
PANK: "The Trumpet Player" and "Long Suffering"
Poets Reading the News: "Unreal"
Sugar House Review: "Earthquake Sensors Record Unprecedented Drop in Human Activity Due to Pandemic"
The Good Men Project: "What I Meant," "In Europe, Mothers Enjoy Two Years of Maternity Leave," and "I Buried the Workweek" (nominated for the Pushcart Prize)
The Journal: "I Said Screen Time Is Over in One More Minute"
The Pinch: "Whales Keep Carbon Out of the Atmosphere"
The 2River View: "My Son Distrusts People Who Are Happy All the Time"
Two Hawks Quarterly: "Placenta"

In addition, the poems "Mandatory Palestine," "I Buried the Workweek,"

"In Europe, Mothers Enjoy Two Years of Maternity Leave," "There Was a Man Named Job," and "The Front Gates of the Jewish Graveyard in Cairo" are available from Pen & Anvil Press as a set of printed broadsides.

I recognize that Waltham, where I live and work, is the unceded territory of the Massachusett people, stewards of this land for hundreds of generations.

We are all dependent on one another in this world — we can't do it alone.

Thank you so much, Eileen Cleary, for creating a community of poets, the Lily Poetry Salon, where this book could imagine being born, nourished by a whole village of inspiration and wisdom. I am grateful for your vision, your compassion, and your intellect. Eileen is not only a wonder of small-press publishing but among the finest people the world has ever made, and I am honored to regard her not only as my publisher but as a friend. Thank you as well to Christine Jones, whose editorial eye helped hone these poems into their final form; to Martha McCollough for her wonderful design work; and to Kristin Kelley for proofreading. Vast thanks to my mentor poets and blurb writers, whose words humble me every time I read them again.

It's amazing that my writing crew from college continues to uplift and support me. I am thankful to Zachary Bos for hosting a workshop where folks gathered to read and respond to early drafts of the "Jerusalem" poems, and for designing a beautiful set of broadsides at Pen & Anvil Press that hung for a few sweet months at my synagogue, Congregation Dorshei Tzedek. Often the first person I think of to send a draft, Georgy Cohen, you read some of these poems way before they were published. James Fleming, you have been telling me I'm a writer since I met you, and never say no to a "will you read this" text. Thank you for your many thoughtful comments and for your friendship over the years.

I'm grateful to Matthew Lippman for your early encouragement as I began to write again, and for your feedback on this manuscript as it took shape. I also want to thank Andrew Sofer for reading through the manuscript and offering valuable wit and wisdom; Cheryl Clark-Vermeulen for teaching the class on ending writer's block at Cambridge Center for Adult Education that did indeed end my long drought; and Kevin McLellan for creating a workshop space in your apartment that allowed me to be myself and improve my craft.

This book wouldn't exist without Rabbi Toba Spitzer, who is a marvel in so many ways it would take a whole book to list them all. You taught me the concept of "God as metaphor," and your many thoughtful dvarim and midrashim sparked me to ask the big questions — and be OK with not knowing the answers. Equally valuable were the conversations I had with Dorshei members at kiddush lunch or while waiting for my kids to get in trouble at Hebrew school. You allowed me to allow myself to become a Jewish poet, whatever that means.

Some of these pieces were written in direct response to the news and began life as a quote from a *New York Times* or *NPR* or *Economist* story. I am grateful to the journalists who cover the protests, wars, and lives of Palestians, Israelis, and Americans directly involved at the source of these poems. Special thanks too for those working toward nonviolent solutions, such as Combatants for Peace, whose emissaries spoke at my synagogue and hosted our rabbi and congregation many times. It is incredibly moving and hopeful to hear from Palestinians and Israelis who "raised weapons which they aimed at each other and saw each other only through gun sights" demonstrate through action that there is a real alternative to the cycle of violence.

To my midwife, Audra, whose excellence can only be hinted at in these poems, profound gratitude and appreciation for your presence and acumen during the most intense period of my life so far. I continue to be in awe of your skill and serenity.

Shout-out to my BFFs, the JEVA Sanity Squad — Erica, Val, and Amy — you have hearts and brains the size of mountains and keep reminding me what's at stake, and I'll love you forever. Thank you for every hug, every call, and all your warmth and support!

Deep love and thanks to my parents, Barbara and Murray, for engendering my Jewish identity, for your support of my writing poems, and for double-checking all the dates and family details in this collection.

And last but not least, I am kvelling with joy that my husband and children don't mind being characters in this narrative, and I'm filled with gratitude for your patience and humor as I wrote these poems and put together this book.

About the author

Author photo credit: Ken Marcou

Josette Akresh-Gonzales lives in the Boston area with her husband and two boys and rides her bike to work at a nonprofit medical publisher. Her work has been published in *The Southern Review, The Indianapolis Review, JAMA, The Pinch, The Journal, Breakwater Review, PANK,* and many other journals. A recent poem has been included in the anthology *Choice Words* (Haymarket). She co-founded the journal *Clarion* and was its editor for two years. Website: josettepoet.com. Tweets @Vivakresh.

www.ingramcontent.com/pod-product-compliance
Lightning Source LLC
Chambersburg PA
CBHW031256120626
46545CB00007B/2838